Anonymous

Presentation of Regimental Colors to the Legislature

Anonymous

Presentation of Regimental Colors to the Legislature

ISBN/EAN: 9783743313316

Manufactured in Europe, USA, Canada, Australia, Japa

Cover: Foto ©ninafisch / pixelio.de

Manufactured and distributed by brebook publishing software
(www.brebook.com)

Anonymous

Presentation of Regimental Colors to the Legislature

(CIRCULAR.)

General Head-Quarters—State of New York.

ADJUTANT GENERAL'S OFFICE,
ALBANY, *January* 21, 1863.

In connection with instructions from these Head-Quarters, dated Albany, N. Y., December 2d, 1862, Commanders of New York State troops, in the field, are desired to transmit an annual return of casualties in the following form, commencing January 1st, 1862, and ending December 31st, 1862. The following will be adhered to as closely as possible:

Strength of regiment January 1, 1862.	Recruits received during the year.	Killed in battle.	Died from diseases, wounds, and other causes.	Actions in which the regiment has participated.

It is desired that all regimental colors, worn out in service, and of consolidated regiments, be forwarded to these Head-Quarters, as well as captured flags, banners, &c., that they may be deposited in the archives of the State, in an appropriate manner, as a record of the valor and fortitude of her sons. A minute history of the flags is important, and a detailed statement of the services of the regiment will be appropriate.

JOHN T. SPRAGUE,

Adjutant General.

BUREAU OF MILITARY STATISTICS.

The Legislature of this State has recently made provision for obtaining, and preserving in permanent form, the history of New York troops engaged in the present war. The plan contemplates the collection of documents and records pertaining to regiments and other commands, and, as far as possible, an authentic sketch of every person in the State who has volunteered into the service of the General Government since the 15th day of April, 1861. The records of the services of the several regiments will, so far as possible, include an account of their organization, and subsequent history and operations, together with an account of the aid, in men and means, afforded by the several towns, cities and counties of the State towards the prosecution of the present war.

It is intended to form a collection of the flags of regiments, as they may from time to time be replaced by new ones, or as the regiments are consolidated or mustered out, and to preserve such trophies and relics as may be procured. As extensive a collection as possible will be made of biographical notices, journals, narratives, published documents, correspondence and original papers. These will be carefully kept for future reference and use, under such regulations as may be deemed necessary for their safety. Such photographic or other portraits of officers or privates as may be contributed to the collection, will be indexed and bound, or otherwise preserved.

The active co-operation of officers and soldiers now, or formerly in the public service, is respectfully solicited in increasing the collections already begun. To facilitate preservation, manuscripts prepared for this office should be written upon common sized foolscap paper, using, if practicable, but one side, and always allowing an inch margin on the left hand side. When equally convenient, photographs upon paper are preferable to portraits taken upon glass or metal; they may then be easily preserved in volumes prepared for the purpose. The united efforts of our citizens, both in and out of the public service, may, it is hoped, form a collection that will acquire an interest and value commensurate with the mag 'tude and importance of the subject, and present a lasting evidence of the pàtriotic efforts of the people of the State of New York in the preservation of the Union, to which they have ever been constantly and earnestly devoted.

All communications or donations intended for this purpose should be addressed to

Col. LOCKWOOD L. DOTY,

Chief of Bureau of Military Statistics,

Albany, N. Y.

In Assembly, Thursday, *April 23d*, 1863.

Mr. McLean offered, for the consideration of the House, a resolution in the words following, to wit:

"Whereas, there are now in the possession of the Adjutant General of this State a number of national and regimental flags, which have been gallantly borne by our brave volunteer regiments until, blood-dyed and torn, they are no longer of use in the field; therefore,

"*Resolved*, That a respectful message be sent to the Honorable the Senate, inviting them to a joint meeting with this House, to be held in the Assembly Chamber on Friday, 24th inst., at 12 o'clock M., His Excellency the Governor presiding, when the Adjutant General will present these flags to the State for preservation."

Mr. Speaker put the question whether the House would agree to said resolution, and it was determined in the affirmative.

In Assembly, *April 24th*, 1863.

The hour of 12 o'clock having arrived,

Mr. Davis moved that a committee be appointed to wait upon the Honorable the Senate and inform them that the House are ready for joint meeting.

11

Mr. SPEAKER put the question whether the House would agree to said motion, and it was determined in the affirmative.

Mr. SPEAKER appointed Messrs. DAVIS and WEAVER as such committee.

Mr. DEPEW moved that a like committee be appointed to wait upon the Governor.

Mr. SPEAKER put the question whether the House would agree to said motion, and it was determined in the affirmative.

Mr. SPEAKER appointed as such committee Messrs. DEPEW and VAN BUREN.

Mr. BOSTWICK moved the appointment of a committee to wait upon the Adjutant General.

Mr. SPEAKER put the question whether the House would agree to said motion, and it was determined in the affirmative.

Mr. SPEAKER appointed Messrs. BOSTWICK and MARSHALL as such committee.

At the same time corresponding proceedings took place in the Senate, viz:

IN SENATE, *April* 24*th*, 1863.

A message was sent by the Assembly, inclosing the above resolution of Mr. McLEAN, and

Mr. SMITH moved that the Senate consent to the meeting proposed in said resolution.

The President put the question whether the Senate would agree to said motion, and it was determined in the affirmative.

Mr. DAVIS and Mr. WEAVER, a committee from the Assembly, appeared and announced that the Assembly was now ready to meet the Senate in joint convention, in pursuance of the resolution heretofore adopted for the purpose of receiving on behalf of the State the national flags in the possession of the Adjutant General of the State.

The Sergeant-at-Arms of the Assembly then appeared at the bar of the House and announced the appearance of committees of the House, with the Governor, the Senate and Adjutant General of the State.

The Assembly rose, and the Senators took seats in front of the Speaker's desk, the Governor occupying the chair, with Lieut. Governor DAVID R. FLOYD JONES on his right, and the Speaker of the Assembly, the Hon. THEOPHILUS C CALLICOT, on his left.

Adjutant General SPRAGUE then advanced to the Speaker's desk, followed by seven flags, borne by members of his Staff, amidst the enthusiastic applause of the House and audience.

After the convention had been called to order by Governor SEYMOUR, the flags being arranged in front of the Speaker's desk,

Adjutant General SPRAGUE spoke as follows :

" These mute but expressive monitors speak a language of their own, leaving but little for me to say. They come here breathing the fervid eloquence of patriotism, of loyalty, gallantry, fortitude, and fidelity to our country and to the Union ; they come from battle fields warm with the blood of our countrymen. As this assemblage gazes upon them, with hearts overflowing with emotion, how little can those who have not been associated, appreciate the trials and toils of those men, who have fought under and around these banners, contending with a fierce and vigilant foe, who, with unrelenting prejudice and vindictive hate, are struggling to destroy this Government, which, for so many years, has secured to us prosperity and happiness, and commanded the respect of the civilized world.

"While our hearts are sad, as well as grateful, we feel a spirit of exultation and pride that, though these banners have come back torn, tattered and soiled, they have never been dishonored, and have been carried by bold, patriotic and intrepid men through the fierce conflict, and have come forth with victory perched upon their eagles.

" Very near do these returning colors come to hearthstones of the citizens of this State—to many within the sound of my voice. Fathers, mothers, brothers and sisters, once followed them to the camp, and with sorrowful, but with willing hearts, bid God speed to those whose affections clustered around the domestic hearthstone.

"Many weary days and nights have they watched the wavering storm of battle, though distant, but in painful reality, as its surging wave broke at the domestic fireside. The colors have returned, but many of the followers are left; and as we recount their noble deeds, the parent's heart warms with a glow of gratitude and pride that they had a son whose noble example has won the love of his countrymen, and who has given a guaranty of the perpetuity of our Union. Yes! these banners are greeted with warmth and affection; cherished relatives and friends have not lived to return with them, but in their absence we embrace the standards and kiss their eagles.

"My task is done. I now commit to you, sir, as the Commander-in-Chief of the State of New York, these banners, in compliance with the request of the officers mentioned, knowing that they will be cherished by the State, as all others will be now in the field.

"When you and I, sir, shall have passed away, when this vast assemblage, now heaving with emotion, shall be mingled with the dust, these mementoes will live ; history will claim its triumph, when the integrity and sacrifices of our countrymen will be appreciated, understood and rewarded.

"Let there be selected by this united body a suitable depository ; there let them hang, so that in time to come, when our country is restored to its original purity and greatness, when rebellion shall be crushed, our children's children shall gather under the folds, and with pride and enthusiasm narrate the deeds of their fathers, and glory in the sacrifices and sorrows which achieved the restitution of our country."

General SPRAGUE then designated the respective colors presented, as follows, each color being waved as it was mentioned :

COLORS OF THE 30th REGIMENT N. Y. S. V.

Col. FRISBY, of Albany, originally commanded this regiment, which was raised in Washington, Albany, Rensselaer, Saratoga, Warren, Columbia and Dutchess counties, comprising at date of departure, June 24th, 1861, 800 men.

This regiment participated in the battles of FALMOUTH, RAPPAHANNOCK CROSSING, GAINESVILLE, GROVETON, BULL RUN (2d), SOUTH MOUNTAIN, ANTIETAM and FREDERICKSBURG.

At the last battle of Bull Run these colors fell during the engagement in the hands of ten different soldiers, shot dead on the field. Thirty-six balls passed through the Stars and Stripes, and the staff was shot into splinters. Two hundred men out of three hundred and forty-one were killed or wounded; fourteen out of seventeen line officers fell upon the field; among them was Col. EDWARD FRISBY, of Albany.

This regiment was mustered into the United States service 800 strong. At the battle of Antietam but forty-nine officers and men reported for

3

duty; it now comprises of the old soldiers twenty-seven officers and men—all that now remain for duty of the original members. Three stand of colors were captured from the enemy at the battle of South Mountain, and at Antietam four flags were captured.

Col. WILLIAM M. SEARING commanded this regiment, and Lieut. Col. M. H. CHRYSLER now transmits these colors from the field, to be presented to the State of New York.

COLORS OF THE 40th REGIMENT N. Y. S.V.

This regiment was originally commanded by Col. EDWARD J. RILEY, of New York city, and is known as

"THE MOZART REGIMENT,"

and was raised in the city of New York, comprising at date of departure, July 4th, 1861, 1039 men.

Col. THOMAS W. EGAN now commands the regiment, and transmits this flag to be presented to the State of New York. A minute history of the colors has not as yet been received.

COLORS OF THE 60th REGIMENT N. Y. S. V.

This regiment, known as

"THE OGDENSBURGH REGIMENT,"

was originally commanded by Col. WM. B. HAY-WARD, who soon after resigned, and was raised in St. Lawrence county, comprising at date of departure, November 4th, 1861, 1000 men.

Lieut. Col. J. C. O. REDDINGTON is now in command of this regiment, which, at present, numbers about 600 men. It has participated in the battle of CEDAR MOUNTAIN, where thirty men were killed and seventy-three wounded. Four of the Color Guard were shot down on the field while bearing their colors. The regiment held the field until their ammunition was exhausted, the men using the cartridges and guns of the dead and wounded. The regiment was commanded here by Major J. E. LANE. This regiment participated in the battles of the last BULL RUN, SULPHUR SPRINGS and ANTIETAM, in which it lost sixty-three in killed and wounded.

Lieut. Col. J. C. O. REDDINGTON transmits the banner, to be deposited with the State.

COLORS OF THE 61st REGIMENT N. Y. S. V.

This regiment is known as

"THE CLINTON GUARD,"

and was originally commanded by Col. SPENCER H. CONE. It was raised in the city of New York in October, 1861, and comprised at the date of departure, November 10th, 1861, 831 men.

Its flag has been borne through the battles of YORKTOWN, FAIR OAKS, PEACH ORCHARD, SAVAGE STATION, WHITE OAK SWAMP, CHARLES CITY CROSS-ROADS, ANTIETAM, MALVERN HILL, CHARLESTOWN, SNICKER'S GAP and FREDERICKSBURG.

At the battle of Fair Oaks four officers were killed and four wounded. One hundred and twelve were killed and wounded. The Color Bearer, with four of the Color Guard, were killed on the field.

At Peach Orchard and Savage Station one.

At White Oak Swamp two commissioned officers and twelve men were killed.

At Charles City Cross-roads six commissioned officers were severely wounded, and over fifty men were killed and wounded. One flag was taken from a Georgia regiment, inscribed with "Williamsburgh" and "Seven Pines."

At Malvern Hill fifty men were killed and wounded.

At Antietam the regiment went into action only two hundred strong; captured two flags from the enemy, and took about three hundred prisoners.

At Fredericksburg forty men were killed and wounded.

The flag is now sent by Col. NELSON A. MILES from the field, to be presented to the State of New York.

COLORS OF THE 71st REGIMENT N. Y. S.V.,
OR "SECOND EXCELSIOR REGIMENT."

This regiment was organized in the city of New York, and originally commanded by Col. GEORGE B HALL, comprising at the date of their departure, August 18th, 1861, 900 men.

It effected the successful raid at STAFFORD COURT HOUSE, and participated in the battles of FAIR OAKS, CHARLES CITY CROSS-ROADS. MALVERN HILL, BRISTOW STATION, BULL RUN (2d), CHANTILLY and FREDERICKSBURG.

The colors are now transmitted from the field by Col. CHAS. B. HALL, commanding the regiment.

COLORS OF THE 101st REGIMENT N. Y. S. V.

This regiment was originally commanded by Col. EURICO FARDELLA, but has been consolidated with the 37th N. Y. V., and was raised in Onondaga and Delaware counties, and was comprised at the date of departure, March 9th, 1862, of 1000 men.

It participated in the battles of SEVEN PINES, PEACH ORCHARD, SAVAGE STATION, CHICAHOMINY SWAMP, WHITE OAK SWAMP, CHARLES CITY CROSS-ROADS, MALVERN HILL, GROVETON, BULL RUN (2d), CHANTILLY and FREDERICKSBURG.

The colors are now transmitted from the field, through the hands of the Adjutant of the regiment, Lieut. RICHARD P. EAGAN, to be deposited in the State.

COLORS OF THE 102d REGIMENT N. Y. S. V.

This regiment is known as

"THE VAN BUREN LIGHT INFANTRY,"

and was originally commanded by Col. THOMAS B. VAN BUREN, who soon after resigned. It was raised in the city of New York, and comprised at the date of departure, March 8th, 1862, 840 men.

This regiment participated in the DEFENCE OF HARPER'S FERRY; in the battles of CEDAR MOUNTAIN and ANTIETAM; in POPE'S RETREAT TO CENTREVILLE; in the SURRENDER OF WINCHESTER, and in the battle of WHITE SULPHUR SPRINGS.

It has lost two officers killed in battle, and forty-nine men killed and wounded.

The colors are now transmitted by Col. JAS. C. LANE, commanding the regiment, to be deposited with the State.

Senator Smith offered the following resolutions:

The People of the State of New York, represented in Senate and Assembly, in joint convention do hereby tender to their volunteers in the service of the United States their deepest gratitude for the sacrifices which these patriotic men have made in leaving their firesides and their employments at home, to sustain the honor and integrity of the Union.

Resolved, That we will uphold our armies in the field, and sustain at home the families and the rights and interests of our volunteers in the service of the United States until the Union shall be restored, and until the flag of our country shall float again on every fort and in every harbor, town, city, and hamlet in the States now in rebellion against the General Government.

Resolved, That the flags which have been this day presented by the Adjutant General in the presence of the Executive and Legislative departments of this State, and which have been so gallantly borne in battle, be accepted and placed among the archives of the State in the Bureau of Military Statistics, now in charge of Col. Doty, and be preserved as memorials of that eternal vigilance which is the price of liberty.

Resolved, That a copy of these resolutions, and of the proceedings of this joint convention of the Senate and Assembly, be transmitted by his Excellency the Governor, to the commandant of each regiment and separate corps or battalion of volunteers from this State, now in the service of the United States.

Mr. FOLGER, Senator from the 26th (Ontario) district, said:

YOUR EXCELLENCY—I should have preferred to have sat here, a sad and silent spectator of these interesting proceedings, rather than to have taken an active participation in them; for, to my mind, the sensations excited by the scene we now behold, are sorrowful and despondent.

I have seen many flags of regiments go out of this State to the seat of war, attractive and beautiful in the shining lustre of their silken folds, and the glitter of their untarnished eagles, and doubly attractive and beautiful from the heartfelt aspirations for success which went with them, and the hallowed associations which clung to them as symbols of our country's nationality. I have seen them go out, borne by the young and gallant, the ardent in their country's cause, and surrounded by the friends and relatives of the departing brave, and fanned by the cheers and hearty God-speeds of the community which they were leaving. Such a scene had much of exciting exultation in it. It seemed, that going in so just a cause, borne by such brave and patriotic youth, and favored by the good wishes and prayers of such loyal communities, that they went only to certain and speedy victory. But never, until to-day, have I seen any of these colors come back, frayed and torn by the rude elements, and pierced by the ruder hostile missile, and with blood spots and battle rents upon them. They come back, but not in the hands which carried them forth; not surrounded by the stout hearts who left with them, and who defended them in many a day of peril; but they come in the hands of strangers to all their eventful history, and surrounded by those who have shed no blood and dared no peril in their defence.

And, sir, it is difficult, in the rush of feeling which fills the heart, to control one's impulses, and to collect such words and sentiments as are appropriate to be uttered and used in this place on such an occasion; for, as your Adjutant General has read the stories of these flags, and uttered the familiar names of the bloody fields where they have been so gallantly upheld and pushed forward, and has related the fate of the brave men who have borne then thought after thought, and

memory after memory, of those whom I have
known, who have laid down their lives in this
fierce war, have fallen into my mind, until, like a
vase of water, into which pebbles are slowly and
silently dropped, my surcharged heart has near
run over at my eyes. And high above all the
applauding uproar, with which this chamber is
filled, there comes a sound from every city and
village, and hamlet, and cross-road, and solitary
farm house, in all this broad commonwealth, which
fills my ear and penetrates my soul. It is the
wail of women, and the sadder, deeper accompa-
niment of the sob of men; it is the wail of the
widow, and of the fatherless, and of the childless,
and of the bereaved in every relation of life; it
is America weeping for her children and refusing
to be comforted because they are not.

Oh! my country! truly the great and awful
God has laid his heavy hand in hot displeasure
upon thee, and it needs a sublime faith in his far-
seeing and far-ordaining Providence to look on
through the lengthening vista, shot athwart by
the storm of battle, and dim with shower of blood,
and to see in the far distance a re-established

Union, a restored Constitution, a renewed nationality, fresh of life and pure from wrong.

You, sir, will recollect, familiar as you are with all classic allusion, the verse of the Latin poet, that "sentiments sent through the ear, more slowly affect the mind, than impressions subjected to the lively eyes." Thus we, who have remained at home, and ever since these hostilities began, have heard and read of the sufferings, the heroic actions and determined valor of our soldiers, have, perhaps, supposed that we appreciated them and realized the wearing trials, the days and nights of toil and exposure, and the imminent peril of the battle field, thick-set with the chances of death. But the sight of these tattered and blood-stained colors, in which we may perceive what the elements have done, and what the bullet has done upon them, brings home more vividly than any written or spoken words, the trials and the bravery of the devoted men who have borne them through many a field of battle, and defended them from many a fierce assault. Silent they stand here before us, but they tell a tale which stirs the imagination more than any recital.

And, sir, tarnished in their material substance, and battered as they are, with their gloss and glitter long since gone, they have a glory and a lustre far greater than tongue can express. Looking at them, and recalling to mind the names of those fields of heroic steadfastness and daring, where they have been planted and maintained, the soul swells, as if with a share of the lofty gallantry, of the men who stood beneath and about them, and dared death, and often met death, to preserve them from disgrace, and to add to their honor and renown; and the soul goes out, in great gratitude to the men who, zealous and patriotic, have filled the ranks of the nation's armies, and stood her living bulwarks in the time of her sore trial We revere the memory of the soldiers of the revolution; we honor the soldiers of the later war with Britain ; and I fondly believe, that in the coming era, the generations shall be taught in equal measure to revere and honor the soldiers of the Constitution, the defenders of the nationality of the greater commonwealth.

And, sir, this scene teaches us a lesson by which we here, as representatives and public servants,

may well profit. We have been engaged during
the session, now about to close, in fierce party
strife, and in strenuous struggle for mere personal
interests, and have too much neglected those
graver matters, and more vital questions, which
the perils and sufferings of the nation should have
forced upon us. It is well, that in these last
days of the session, these silent monitors should
come to shame us, and to admonish us that we
are engaged in a struggle that should unite all
men, to the abnegation of party, and of private
interests, in the defence of a common country;
and that, abandoning party strife, and laying
aside personal matters and aims, we should
emulate the devotion of the brave men who have
borne these flags through the fields of real battle.
Let us take this lesson to heart, and while we at
home can but feebly realize the trials and the
dangers of those who are actively engaged in this
fearful strife, let us, so far as in our power is, labor
here for the same end to which they are devoted,
the salvation of the country, the re-establishment
of the Union, and the preservation of our nationality. Thus may we best honor the noble men

who have filled our armies and sustained the glory of our arms

I second the motion that these resolutions be adopted.

Hon. T. C. FIELDS, of New York, said:

YOUR EXCELLENCY—I think that every member of this joint convention of the Legislature of the State of New York, and every one of this vast concourse of interested spectators, will recognize the truth, the beauty, and the pertinency of the soul-stirring remarks made by the Adjutant General, and of the polished and feeling response of the accomplished Senator. But, sir, there is not an individual who has witnessed this sad, solemn and impressive ceremony, but must feel that while these war-wrecked and blood-stained banners come to us as symbols of the bravery of the patriotic men who have gone forth from their homes to fight the battle for the Union, and tell us mutely but eloquently the thrilling story of the fierce and cruel strife through which they have been borne with so much honor and devotion—they come to us, also, as painful evidence that our beloved country, once so great, so prosperous and so noble; the home of freedom, the

5

nursery of the arts, the hope of the oppressed, the
model Government of the world—is shaking and
reeling and rocking in the very throes and agony
of dissolution. We should read the solemn lesson
of this scene with but slight advantage, did we
fail to be impressed with this sorrowful fact.
Let us, then, here, to-day, as American citizens
gathered in presence of a joint convention of the
Legislature of the leading State in the Union,
presided over by a Governor who lives in the
hearts of the people, and whose noble sentiments
have stirred the soul of the nation—let us here,
to-day, renew and reconsecrate our devotion to
our country. Let us, to-day, solemnly declare,
what every man here present feels in the inmost
depths of his heart, that we will support the
Government in all constitutional, proper and
vigorous measures to prosecute this war for the
suppression of a wicked rebellion, the restoration
of the Union, and the vindication of the Constitution and the laws!

Let us pledge ourselves, that whatever we have
of strength, of energy, of intellect, of ability, we
will bring it here to-day, and lay it upon the
altar, and consecrate it to the service of our

country! But while we do this, let us upon the bended knees of our broken hearts, beseech the God who rules over our beloved and stricken land, that He will again, and speedily, reunite us as one people and one government; that stretching forth His hand in mercy, and not in wrath, He will calm the angry passions of the human heart, and say to the fierce waves of strife—"Peace, be still!"

Lieut. Gov. JONES, President of the Senate, said:

YOUR EXCELLENCY AND GENTLEMEN OF THE SENATE AND ASSEMBLY—At this stage of the proceedings, allow me to read the following beautiful poem, from the pen of one of America's most accomplished and favorite poets, ALFRED B. STREET:

OUR UNION.

Our Union, the gift of our fathers!
  In wrath roars the tempest above!
The darker and nearer our danger,
  The warmer and closer our love.
Though stricken, it never shall perish;
  It bends, but not breaks to the blast;
Foes rush on in fury to rend it,
  But we will stand true to the last

Our Union, ordained of Jehovah!
  Man sets not the fiat aside;
As well cleave the welkin asunder
  As the one mighty system divide.

The grand Mississippi sounds ever,
  From pine down to palm, the decree;
The spindle, the corn, and the cotton,
  One pæan, shout, Union, to thee!

Our Union, the lightning of battle
  First kindled the flame of its shrine!
The blood and the tears of our people
  Have made it forever divine.
In battle we then will defend it!
  Will fight till the triumph is won!
Till the States form the realm of the Union
  As the sky forms the realm of the sun.

Governor SEYMOUR said:

GENTLEMEN OF THE SENATE AND ASSEMBLY—I can add, by no words of mine, to this impressive and solemn scene. You have heard from a Representative of the Senate, and from a Member of the Assembly of the State. You have listened to the earnest words of one who, himself a soldier, can with so much truth and eloquence depict the dangers and the heroism of a soldier's life. You have heard, too, the beautiful thought and musical language of the poet. But above all, you have seen the banners, which, but a short time since, were carried forth in all their brightness and their beauty, borne by stalwart men, who went out from their happy homes to fight the battles of their country, brought back to us blood-stained and torn, and telling us more eloquently than can any language, of the heroism and devotion of their defenders.

Alas! for the unreturning brave! Alas! that so few of those who fought beneath the folds of these flags, are left to tell their history as they come forth from the terrible strife defaced and tattered, but more dear to us than in their original brightness and beauty.

I will not weaken the effect of this touching and impressive ceremony by any farther remarks. May Almighty God, in His goodness, grant that the heavy sacrifices we have made, may not be in vain; but that with patriotism quickened and elevated by the trials we have undergone, we may be taught to better appreciate and more faithfully discharge the duties of American citizens; and may He, who holds all nations in the hollow of His hand, pardoning our many sins, restore to us our glorious and beloved Union, so that we may again enjoy the blessings of peace, beneath a Government reinvigorated and strengthened by the deep sorrows and the fierce struggle through which it has passed.

Gentlemen of the Senate and Assembly, it now only remains for me to put the question upon the resolutions presented to this joint convention by Senator Smith.

The resolutions were then, by a unanimous vote, adopted.

Hon. GILBERT DEAN, of New York, said:

YOUR EXCELLENCY—I have been a silent spectator of this impressive ceremony, and would have remained so but for the omission of any provision for the official publication of what has here occurred. The involuntary tribute paid in tears, so freely shed by manly eyes, at the sight of these torn and soiled emblems of American nationality, attest the deep and ineradicable devotion of our people to their Government, and demand that a record should be made of the event.

The brave men who, at the summons of honor and of duty, have gone forth to uphold the national authority, should know the sentiments of the people of the State, as embodied and expressed at its Capitol.

Here, to day, both branches of the Legislature, representing the entire people, in the presence of the Executive of their choice and with his concurrence, have solemnly and unanimously resolved that whatever differences may exist as to the causes of the present position of public affairs— as to the manner of conducting the war—or the propriety of this or that administrative measure— under no circumstances can or will the *State of New York consent to a dissolution of this Union.* (Applause.) That to prevent it every energy shall be exerted, and the illimitable means and unbounded resources of the State shall be applied. Let this solemn declaration, and the manner in which these flags have been received, be read by the officer in his quarters; by the soldier on his lonely picket post, or by the light of his camp-fire. It will cheer and encourage; it will stimulate the heart and nerve the arm, as it tells to each that, while his toils and sacrifices are appreciated, and his memory cherished at home, the object for which he forfeits domestic comfort and imperils life is the noblest that ever summoned christian soldier to the field—NATIONAL UNITY—that, though in the struggle he may fall, yet the sacred symbol passed from dying hands to surviving comrades will be preserved, red with patriot blood, effulgent with the glorious achievements of a citizen osldiery, and will be deposited in the archives of the State, there to be preserved among its choicest treasures. Let us not confine these proceedings to the narrow boundaries of this chamber, but send them abroad, so that at least every volunteer from the State of New York shall know what has been said and done here to-day; for that purpose I move that there be printed under the supervision of the Governor and Adjutant General two hundred thousand copies of the proceedings of the joint convention of the Legislature, and the presentation of flags by the Adjutant General to the State, in the presence of the Governor, Senate and Assembly, including the remarks of the speakers, (on superfine paper, with paper covers), the usual number to be furnished to the members, officers and reporters of each House, and a copy to be sent by the Governor to each of the volunteers from this State; the residue, if any, to be deposited in the Bureau of Military Statistics for future use.

The motion was then adopted.

Governor SEYMOUR then declared the joint convention dissolved, and the Governor, the Adjutant General and Senate withdrew from the chamber.

Hon. JAMES DARCY, of Kings, when the House was again called to order, said:

Mr. SPEAKER—In honor of the proceedings of the joint convention, I move that the House now take a recess till 4 o'clock.

The motion was unanimously agreed to, and the House took a recess.

HISTORY OF THE NATIONAL FLAG.

The most interesting incident connected with the battle of Saratoga was the unfurling, for the first time, the Stars and Stripes at the surrender of Burgoyne.

Bunker Hill was fought under a red flag, bearing the motto, "Come, if you dare!" but on the 14th of June, 1777, the Continental Congress resolved "That the flag of the thirteen United States be thirteen stripes, alternate red and white, and that the Union be thirteen stars, white on a blue field, representing a new constellation."

This was made public on the 3d of September following. Previous to this our national banner was the Union flag, combining the crosses of St George and St. Andrew (taken from the English banner) with thirteen stripes, alternate red and white. The banner of St. Patrick (Ireland's emblem) was not combined with the crosses of St. George and St. Andrew in the standard of Great Britain until 1801, the year of the union with Ireland.

The stars of the new flag represented the new constellation of States, the idea taken from the constellation Lyra, which signifies harmony. The blue of the field was taken from the Covenanters' banner in Scotland, likewise significant of the league and covenant of the United Colonies against oppression, and incidentally involving vigilance, perseverance and justice. The stars were disposed in a circle, symbolizing the perpetuity of the Union, the circle being the sign of eternity. The thirteen stripes showed, with the stars, the number of the United Colonies, and denoted the subordination of the States to, and their dependence upon the Union, as well as equality among themselves. The whole was a blending of the various flags previous to the Union flag, viz: the red flags of the army and white ones of the floating batteries—the germ of our navy. The red color, also, which in Roman days was the signal of defiance, denoted daring, and the white purity.

What eloquence do the Stars and Stripes breathe, when their full significance is known! A new constellation; union; perpetuity; a covenant against oppression; equality; subordination; courage; purity.

By the United States law of January 13, 1794, it was enacted "that, from and after the first of May, 1795, the flag of the United States shall be fifteen stripes, alternate red and white," and "that the Union be fifteen stars, white in a blue field." This was our national flag during the war of 1812.

On the 4th of April, 1818, Congress altered the flag, by directing a return to the thirteen stripes, as follows:

"Be it enacted, etc., That from and after the 4th day of July next, the flag of the United States be thirteen horizontal stripes, alternate red and white; that the Union be twenty stars, white, in a blue field.

"And be it further enacted, That, on the admission of a new State into the Union, one star be added to the union of the flag; and that such addition shall take effect on the 4th day of July next succeeding such admission."

The return to the thirteen stripes was by reason of the anticipation that the addition of a stripe on the admission of each State would make the flag too unwieldy. The old number of stripes also perpetuated the original number of States of the Union, while the addition of the stars showed the Union in its existing state.

The flag planted by our troops in the city of Mexico, at the conclusion of the Mexican war, bore thirty stars.

The size of the flag for the army is six feet six inches in length, by four feet four inches in width, with seven red and six white stripes. The first seven stripes (four red and three white) bound the square of the blue field for the stars, the stripes extending from the extremity of the field to the end of the flag. The eighth stripe is white, extending partly at the base of the field. The number of stars is thirty-five.

MEMBERS OF THE N. Y. LEGISLATURE, 1863.

Lieut. Gov. D. R. FLOYD JONES, President of the Senate.

SENATORS.

District 1....MONROE HENDERSON.
2....JESSE C. SMITH.
3....HENRY C. MURPHY.
4....CHRISTIAN B. WOODRUFF.
5....CHARLES G. CORNELL.
6....JOHN J. BRADLEY.
7....RICHARD B. CONNOLLY.
8....HEZEKIAH D. ROBERTSON.
9....HENRY R. LOW.
10....JACOB S. FREER.
11....WILLIAM H. TOBEY.
12....RALPH RICHARDS.
13....JOHN V. L. PRUYN.
14....JOSEPH H. RAMSEY.
15....WILLIAM CLARK.
16....RUSSEL M. LITTLE.
17....CHARLES C. MONTGOMERY
18....JAMES A. BELL.
19....ALEXANDER H. BAILEY.
20....GEORGE A. HARDIN.
21....RICHARD K. SANDFORD.
22....ALLEN MUNROE.
23....HENRY A. CLARK.
24....LYMAN TRUMAN.
25....CHAUNCEY M. ABBOTT.
26....CHARLES J. FOLGER.
27....CHARLES COOK.

District 28....Lysander Farrar.
       29....Almanzor Hutchinson.
       30....Wilkes Angel.
       31....John Ganson.
       32....Horace C. Young.

MEMBERS OF ASSEMBLY.

Hon. THEOPHILUS C. CALLICOT, Speaker.

Dist.	Name.	County
	ADGATE, GEORGE - - -	Clinton.
1.	ALLEN, ANDREW L. - -	Cattaraugus.
	ALDRICH, NEWTON - - -	Warren.
	ANDRUS, ALBERT - - -	Franklin.
3.	BEMIS, HORACE - - - -	Steuben.
1.	BENJAMIN, CHARLES A. -	Jefferson.
1.	BOOKSTAVER, JESSE F. - -	Ulster.
6.	BOSWELL, HENRY C. - -	Kings.
2.	BOSTWICK, ELIAS W. - -	Columbia.
1.	BRAND, WILLIAM H. - -	Madison.
3.	BREED, JOSEPH - - - -	Onondaga.
1.	BROCKETT, IRA - - -	Saratoga.
3.	BROWN, WILLIAM - - -	Monroe
1.	BROOKS, WILLIAM - - -	Otsego.
	CHICKERING, JOHN - - -	Lewis.
2.	CHURCH, CORNELIUS A. -	Otsego.
	CLARK, ELIZUR - - - -	Onondaga.
1.	COLLINS, THADDEUS W. -	Wayne.
4.	CONGER, ANSON G. - - -	Erie.
	CORNELL, EZRA - - -	Tompkins.
1.	COURTNEY, ROBERT W. - -	Delaware.
	CRUTTENDEN, ALVAH E. -	Allegany.
2.	CUTLER, JOHN - - - -	Albany.
4.	DARCY, JAMES - - - -	Kings.
	DAVIS, NATHANIEL W. - -	Tioga.
15.	DEAN, GILBERT - - -	New York.
3.	DEPEW, CHAUNCEY M. - -	Westchester.

7

Dist.	Name.	County.
2.	Dewey, Lanson - - -	Ontario.
3.	Dewey, William - - -	Jefferson.
2.	Dow, Albert G. - - -	Cattaraugus.
2.	Doughty, Joseph C. - -	Dutchess.
2.	Durfee, Lemuel - - -	Wayne.
1.	Duryea, Charles T. - -	Queens.
1.	Dutcher, Luther S. - -	Dutchess.
1.	Field, Perez H. - - -	Ontario.
17.	Fields, Thomas C. - -	New York.
2.	Fisher, Francis B. - - -	Chenango.
1.	Fletcher, Benjamin H -	Niagara.
1.	Flynn, Cornelius - - -	New York.
9.	Freeman, David V. - -	New York.
	Frean, Theodore - - -	Richmond.
2.	Gilbert, Francis R. - -	Delaware.
	Gillespie, William - -	Sullivan.
4.	Gover, William C. - -	New York.
	Green, Loren - - - -	Genesee.
	Haring, James S. - - -	Rockland.
2.	Havens, John S. - - -	Suffolk.
	Havens, Palmer E. - -	Essex.
	Heacock, Willard J. - -	Fult. and Hamilton.
	Healy, Byron - - - -	Wyoming.
8.	Hill, Thomas H. - - -	New York.
3.	Hopkins, Timothy A. -	Erie.
2.	Hopkins, Ervin, Jr. - -	Washington.
2.	Houghton, Nathaniel M.	Saratoga.
2.	Hughes, Bernard - - -	Kings.
	Hulett, Charles - - -	Chemung.
14.	Hutchings, Robert C. - -	New York.
3.	Johnson, Samuel E. - -	Kings.
7.	King, Vincent C. - - -	New York.
1.	Kisselbrack, Peter G. -	Columbia.
6.	Korn, Julius - - - -	New York.
2.	Lake, Henry C. - - -	Chautauqua.
	Lawrence, Samuel - - -	Schuyler.

51

Dist.	Name.	County.
2.	LEAMY, DANIEL	New York.
11.	LEDWITH, THOMAS A.	New York.
2.	LE FEVER, JACOB	Ulster.
7.	LESLIE, CHARLES P.	Kings.
2	LOOMIS, HIRAM W.	Oswego.
2.	LOTT, HENRY S.	Queens.
3.	LOUTREL, GEORGE L.	New York.
2.	LOVERIDGE, EDWARD D.	Allegany.
16.	McCANN, MICHAEL	New York.
4.	McDOUGALL, ISAAC	Oneida.
1.	McGONEGAL, GEORGE E.	Monroe.
2.	McGOWAN, ARCHIBALD C.	Herkimer.
1.	McKEON, JAMES	Rensselaer.
	McLEAN, JAMES	Seneca.
	McSHEA, JOHN, Jr.	Schenectady.
2.	MARSHALL, JOHN E.	Westchester.
1.	MATTOON, ABNER C.	Oswego.
	MAYHAM, STEPHEN L.	Schoharie.
2.	MILLER, LEVI	Jefferson.
2.	MORGAN, WILLIAM	Niagara.
	MOULTON, FREEMAN P.	Montgomery.
1.	MUNRO, JAMES M.	Onondaga.
1.	MURPHY, JOHN W.	Erie.
10.	O'BRIEN, DANIEL M.	New York.
4.	OSWALD, WILLIAM L.	Albany.
3.	PALMER, HARVEY	Oswego.
	PARKS, JOHN	Orleans.
3.	PARKER, ABRAHAM X.	St. Lawrence.
1.	PAULDING, JOHN	Kings.
1.	POST, GEORGE I.	Cayuga.
2.	PRESCOTT, DANIEL M.	Oneida.
1.	PRINDLE, ELIZUR H.	Chenango.
2.	QUACKENBUSH, JOHN A.	Rensselaer.
2.	REDINGTON, JAMES	St. Lawrence.
2.	ROBINSON, WILLIAM P.	Cayuga.
	ROE, LUKE	Greene.

Dist.	Name.	County.
5.	Rogers, Henry - - -	New York.
2.	Rouse, George L. - - -	Madison.
2.	Seymour, Horatio - -	Erie.
	Shaw, Guy - - - - - -	Yates.
3.	Sherman, Asa S. - - -	Oneida.
2.	Sherwood, Henry - - -	Steuben.
	Skinner, Samuel - - -	Livingston.
12.	Smith, Andrew - - - -	New York.
1.	Smith, Hamilton E. - -	Livingston.
	Smith, Francis B. - - -	Broome.
	Smith, Saxton - - -	Putnam.
1.	Snyder, William J. - -	Albany.
3.	Strait, Ebenezer S. - -	Rensselaer.
1.	Steward, John - - - -	Chautauqua.
1.	Sweet, Griffin - - -	Herkimer.
1.	Taggart, John W - - -	Steuben.
1.	Talman, Pierre C. - -	Westchester.
1.	Teft, Asa C. - - - -	Washington.
1.	Townsley, Elias P. - -	St. Lawrence.
2.	Trimmer, Eliphaz - - -	Monroe.
1.	Van Buren, John D. - -	Orange.
	Van Hoesen, Henry B. -	Cortland.
3.	Wait, Henry L - - -	Albany.
13.	Ward, Alexander - - -	New York.
1.	Weaver, Abram B. - -	Oneida.
3.	Westbrook, Ebenezer -	Ulster.
1.	Wiggins, Benjamin - -	Suffolk.
2.	Woodward Charles S. -	Orange.

www.ingramcontent.com/pod-product-compliance
Lightning Source LLC
Chambersburg PA
CBHW021434090426
42739CB00009B/1477